A VILLAG"S JOURNEY IN TO POSTIVE THINKING

by srinivasa raya

Acknowledgment: In the kaleido-scopic journey of crafting this book, I extend my deepest gratitude to the village of words, ideas, and inspirations that wove themselves into the fabric of every page. It takes a village to birth a tale, and in this endeavor, I am humbled by the support and contributions that turned mere thoughts into a vibrant narrative.

To the characters who danced through the pages, each with their unique stories and lessons, thank you for allowing me to be a scribe to your adventures. Your resilience, joy, and triumphs added layers to this tale, making it a rich tapestry of the human spirit.

I express heartfelt appreciation to the village of readers who will embark on this journey. Your open hearts and curious minds are the winds beneath the wings of this book, propelling it to soar into the realms of possibilities.

A debt of gratitude is owed to the village of knowledge and wisdom, where the river of ideas flowed generously. The storytellers, philosophers, and poets who paved the roads of understanding positive thinking deserve recognition for their invaluable insights.

I extend thanks to the mentors, guides, and supporters who, like pillars in the village square, provided strength and direction. Your encouragement became the steady banyan tree under which this story found shade.

Last but not least, I acknowledge the village within – the realm of imagination, dreams, and creativity. In this village, boundaries blur, and possibilities are as vast as the sky. It is here that the alchemy of words and ideas transforms the ordinary into the extraordinary.

In the spirit of gratitude, I offer this book to the collective village – a celebration of positivity, resilience, and the unwavering belief that every villager is indeed born to win.

With heartfelt thanks,
SRINIVASA RAYA

Introduction:

Welcome to the enchanting village nestled between the pages of this book – a village that exists not on any map but within the realm of words, thoughts, and shared dreams. Here, under the village banyan tree, we embark on a journey of transformation, guided by the mantra that echoes through the cobblestone paths: "Born to Win."

This book is not a conventional tale but a symphony of stories, a mosaic of wisdom woven together with threads of positivity, resilience, and the magic found in simple moments. In the heart of our village, positive thinking is not a fleeting notion but a way of life – an art to be mastered, a lantern to guide us through stormy nights.

As we wander through the chapters, each one a lantern illuminating a different facet of positive thinking, we'll encounter characters like Raj, Ganesh, Rani, Sundar, and Vijay. Their tales are not distant legends but mirrors reflecting the universal struggles and triumphs we all face.

"Ganesh's Grin" sets the stage, inviting you to explore the village where happiness is found in the laughter of children and the warmth of chai cups. "Rani's Resilience" teaches us to face storms with a smile, while "Sundar's Sunrise" reveals the power of finding light in the darkest nights. "Vijay's Victory" dismantles doubts, and "A Bridge to Tomorrow" invites us to understand the essence of positive thinking.

We'll dance through the festival of "Fun and Games," discovering that learning about positivity can be as joyful as flying a kite on a sunny day. In "Blossoming Souls," we learn the transformative power of respect, and in "Stormy Skies, Steadfast Hearts," we navigate obstacles with the shield of positivity.

As we reach the midpoint with "Dawn After Darkness," we find that avoiding despair is not weakness but a path to resilience. "Guiding Stars in the Night" reveals the lanterns of self-compassion and community support that guide us through the darkest times.

The breaking dawn of "Breaking Dawn" signals the transition to mastering positive thinking, where we explore the goodness within and extend it beyond ourselves. "Radiant Horizons" unveils the ultimate gifts of mastery, and "Wings of Victory" propels us into life's triumph.

In the village's final celebration, we unite under the moonlit sky, embracing the mantra, "You Are Only Born to Win, So Win Your Life." As you turn the pages, may you find not just a story but a companion in your journey – a companion named Positive Thinking.

So, dear reader, let the adventure begin. Walk the cobbled streets, breathe the jasmine-scented air, and let the village unfold its magic, one page at a time. Welcome to the village where every villager is born to win

A Village's Journey into Positive Thinking"

Paint Your Life with Positivity: Where Every Villager is Born to Win

Chapter 1: A New Beginning with Raj

Raj's Radiance

In the tranquil embrace of a village bathed in the ethereal morning glow, our story unfolds with Raj at its center, a young dreamer navigating life's expanse. The sun, casting a golden hue on the grazing cows and whispering trees, sets the stage for our protagonist's journey.

Raj, a canvas painted with aspirations as vast as the open sky and concerns as minuscule as grains of sand, finds himself under the shade of a venerable banyan tree. In this idyllic setting, the narrative takes an unexpected turn when an old, weathered book captures Raj's attention – a book that would become the key to unlocking the magic of positive thinking.

A Glimpse into Positive Thinking

As Raj delves into the dusty pages, grappling with words like a child with untied shoelaces, the book introduces the transformative concept of positive thinking.

The notion that a mere shift in perspective can sweeten life's experiences, akin to the juiciness of a summer mango, takes root in Raj's curious mind. The thematic essence is laid bare – the power of positivity to illuminate even the dreariest of days.

A Seed Planted, Dreams Awakened

With newfound insight, Raj embarks on a subtle metamorphosis. Life's burdens, once as relentless as a monsoon rain, begin to lift. Dreams, once perceived as distant stars, draw closer. The dusty pages of the book act as a sprinkling of fairy dust, igniting a spark within Raj.

As we linger under the banyan tree, savoring chai and weaving tales, Raj's story serves as a precursor to the unfolding journey. Our sojourn into the realm of positive thinking is likened to the subtle yet transformative spice in a grandmother's curry – an ingredient that alters the flavor of life itself. Together, we traverse this path where each step mirrors a leisurely stroll through village fields, and the promise of a positivity-laden dawn looms just beyond the horizon

the Simple Moments - Ganesh's Grin

Having waded through the gentle currents of Raj's tale, we plunge deeper into the narrative, unveiling the core of our expedition in the chapter titled "Ganesh's Grin." Here, we introduce the central tenet of our journey, articulated in a language even the sparrows on village roofs comprehend – "Feeling Happy in Small Moments." This thematic essence resembles a vibrant rangoli, adorning the doorstep of life with splashes of color.

In our journey, we invite you to envision happiness not as a grand Bollywood spectacle but as the subtle, profound joy found in the simplicity of daily life. As we embark on this exploration, put aside scholarly pursuits and imagine we're friends sharing the warmth of freshly cooked samosas.

Meet Ganesh, the sagacious elder of our village, a figure with a perpetual grin not due to overflowing pockets but because he has mastered the art of discovering joy in the ordinary. Happiness, for Ganesh, resides in the bloom of marigolds and the rhythmic tabla beats during village festivities.

Unveiling the Hidden Treasure of Happiness

As Ganesh's story unfolds, we unravel the layers of our theme. Life may not be a Bollywood extravaganza, yet within the tapestry of our daily routines lies a concealed trove of happiness. It's in the laughter of children, the fragrance of jasmine, or the comforting warmth of chai on a rainy day – the simple moments that paint our lives with joy.

Through Ganesh's experiences, we emphasize that this journey is not a pursuit of complex philosophies or adorned with lofty words. Instead, it's an homage to the wisdom of the grinning uncle in our village, a testament that happiness is not a luxury but a fundamental aspect of existence.

Prepare to traverse the realm of Ganesh's grin, where happiness is not an elusive dream but an intrinsic aspect of life. In the unassuming pages that follow, you'll come to understand that positive thinking isn't about grand gestures; it starts with treasuring the small joys that set your heart dancing, much like Ganesh in the village square.

chapter.2 Rani's Resilience -

As we huddle around the village fire, the flames casting a warm glow on eager faces, the tales of ordinary individuals who transformed pain into power unfold. This chapter, titled "Rani's Resilience," unveils stories of strength, with Rani as the harbinger of a powerful lesson – facing pain with a smile.

Rani, with a countenance kissed by the sun and hands bearing the marks of labor, confronted life's tempests like a robust boat navigating stormy seas. Her story stands as a living testament to the transformative power of positive thinking in the midst of adversity.

Amidst clouds heavy with rain and tears cascading from the heavens, Rani's modest abode crumbled one fateful day. Stripped of everything – memories, shelter, and the comforting embrace of her home – Rani stood resilient. Instead of succumbing to despair, she faced the ruins with unwavering determination. With each brick laid, she whispered words of hope and gratitude, transforming her pain into the bedrock for a stronger tomorrow.

The heart of positive thinking beats in Rani's ability to confront pain with a smile, turning adversity into a stepping stone rather than a stumbling block. As we gather by the fire, let's ponder our own challenges, contemplating how, like Rani, we can reshape them into narratives of resilience.

In the gentle warmth of the fire's glow, we won't drench you with heavy words like a monsoon shower. Instead, let's sprinkle the light rain of understanding on the concepts of positive thinking. It's not about denying pain or feigning perpetual sunshine and rainbows. No, it's about acknowledging the storms, feeling the raindrops, and choosing to dance in the rain.

Positive actions, my friend, are as uncomplicated as planting a seed of hope in the soil of despair. As we tread further on this journey, let Rani's resilience be our guide, a beacon as we face our own storms with a smile. In the realm of positive thinking, even the darkest clouds can unravel into stories of triumph

SRINIVASA RAYA AND VILLAGE LIFE IS GOOD

Sundar's Sunrise - Illuminating Darkness with a Whisper of Hope

Beneath the enchanting starlit sky, allow me to share the tale of Sundar, a man whose life took an unexpected turn when the night seemed interminable. His story, far from a sorrowful lament, is a spark of hope that kindled the very fabric of his existence.

Sundar, with hands weathered by life's trials and a heart laden with burdens, found himself ensconced in a pit so profound that even the moonlight struggled to penetrate its depths. It was amidst this shadow of despair that a friend, much like the companions gathered under the celestial canopy, handed him a modest book – akin to the one we are crafting together.

Within those unassuming pages, Sundar unearthed a revelation that acted as a catalyst for change. It wasn't about turning a blind eye to the darkness or feigning its absence. Instead, it was about uncovering a minuscule flicker within, a spark capable of illuminating even the most obscure corners of his life.

This revelation marked Sundar's sunrise, a subtle yet transformative turning point in his journey towards positive thinking. There were no grand fanfares or dramatic crescendos; just a quiet whisper that resonated, affirming, "You can find light even in the darkest night."

As we amble alongside Sundar through the dimly lit village paths, let me sprinkle the starlight of wisdom on you – the proven benefits of positive thinking. Far from a fanciful notion, it is underpinned by the sagacity of collective minds. Scientific research attests that positive thinking serves as a lantern in the night, guiding us through challenges while enhancing our physical well-being.

Studies indicate that a positive mindset can alleviate stress, fortify our immune system, and contribute to a longer, healthier life. It's not sorcery; rather, it's the symphony of heart and mind working in harmonious tandem. So, as we traverse the continuum of our journey, let Sundar's sunrise be etched in our hearts, a testament that positive thinking is not ephemeral but a guiding star woven into the intricate tapestry of our lives.

chapter.3 Vijay's Victory

As we convene around the village well, allow me to unveil the narrative of Vijay, a man who confronted his doubts head-on, wielding the shield of positive thinking to triumph over the shadows that often cloud our minds. Vijay's tale isn't a narrative of capitulation; rather, it's a resounding victory over the doubts that can besiege us.

Now, let's confront a prevalent doubt that might lurk in the recesses of our minds – the notion that positive thinking is merely fanciful daydreaming. Vijay, akin to many, once harbored this misconception. He feared that acknowledging his doubts would equate to surrendering to them. Yet, through his journey, he proved this notion to be unfounded.

Vijay's odyssey commenced when he resolved to face his apprehension of public speaking, a fear capable of turning his knees into jelly at the mere thought. Empowered by the force of positive thinking, Vijay transformed his fear into a stepping stone for personal growth.

Now, here's the practical essence: Vijay didn't wake up one day magically fearless. Instead, he acknowledged his fear, dissected it into more manageable components, and approached each facet with a positive mindset. His journey began modestly – speaking before a mirror, then to a confidant, gradually building the fortress of his confidence.

Positive thinking, for Vijay, wasn't about dismissing the fear; rather, it was about utilizing it as fuel for courage. It's akin to illuminating a dim room, one switch at a time. As we gather by the well, envision yourself standing in Vijay's shoes, confronting a fear with a newfound ally – positive thinking.

Let's wholeheartedly embrace Vijay's victory as our own. As we navigate our fears, regardless of their magnitude, remember that positive thinking isn't about feigning their nonexistence. It's about acknowledging, dissecting, and triumphing over them one courageous step at a time. While the village well may currently resonate with laughter, with each conquest over fear, it will echo the triumphant cheers of those who dared to believe in the potent force of positivity

A Bridge to Tomorrow - Navigating the Landscape of Positive Thinking

In the heart of our village journey, we stand at a pivotal juncture – a bridge that spans the wisdom gathered from Raj's radiance, Sundar's sunrise, and Vijay's victory. This chapter, "A Bridge to Tomorrow," marks the midpoint, beckoning us to reflect on the treasures we've unearthed. Like a bridge connecting two shores, we now step into the terrain of understanding positive thinking.

This segment acts as a compass, simplifying the principles that render positive thinking more than a mere buzzword. No need for cryptic lexicon or clandestine codes; our discourse shall be as straightforward as sharing a cup of chai.

Picture this chapter as a treasure map guiding us through the landscapes of thoughts and emotions. We'll uncover why positive thinking transcends wishful pondering, evolving into a lantern that illuminates our path, even in the darkest nights. Through relatable stories and the sagacity of the village, we shall unveil the secrets behind comprehending positive thinking.

So, dear friend, let us traverse this bridge hand in hand, venturing into the core of positivity. Here, confidentiality isn't about harboring secrets; it's about sharing the intricacies of our hearts, comprehending the murmurings of our minds, and unlocking the door to a realm where positive thinking isn't enigmatic but a steadfast companion.

As we advance, bear in mind that grasping positive thinking mirrors the discovery of a concealed garden in the heart of the village – it burgeons with possibilities, and each step unravels a new petal of wisdom. Let's turn the page together, stepping onto the bridge that leads us to the tomorrow we've been yearning

chapter.4 A Tapestry of Tales

Beneath the sheltering branches of the village banyan tree, let us embark on the chapter titled "A Tapestry of Tales." Here, we interlace vibrant threads of stories from those who embraced positive thinking as a companion on their journey. These narratives, like threads in the fabric of our lives, illuminate the B Story – a collective saga of support, growth, and the enchantment that unfolds when we become supporters of all.

Meet Manju, a spirited woman whose laughter resonated through the village. Her tale unfolds during a period when life's burdens rivaled the weight of a sack of rice. Yet, she discovered that the load could be lightened not only by her own positive thinking but also by being a supporter of all.

Manju's simple acts of kindness, such as adorning the village square with flowers or offering a comforting word to a troubled neighbor, set forth a ripple effect of positivity. Her emotional and personal growth was not a solitary expedition but a communal dance of hearts. The more she supported others, the more she blossomed into a radiant beacon of warmth.

Within this chapter, we immerse ourselves in stories of villagers lifting each other during challenging times, sharing joys, and becoming stalwarts of support. It transcends individual success; it embodies the collective triumph of a community thriving on positivity.

So, let us emulate Manju, sowing seeds of encouragement in the soil of our village hearts. As supporters of all, we shall discover that the growth witnessed in others mirrors our own blossoming. The village banyan tree stands majestic not solely due to its individual branches but because each leaf supports the other, creating a canopy of strength.

In the resonance of these tales, let's retain the essence that positive thinking is not a solitary performance; it's a symphony where every note contributes to the melody. Together, we become the wind beneath each other's wings, soaring higher than we ever could alone

chapter .6 The Gratitude Hunt

Initiate the festivities with the joyful game of The Gratitude Hunt. Villagers embark on a daily adventure, noting three things they're grateful for. Sharing these moments creates a sense of community, transforming ordinary days into celebrations of gratitude.

The Smile Challenge

Dive into the heart of the festival with The Smile Challenge. Villagers are urged to spread positivity by smiling at strangers or friends throughout the day. Counting the smiles in return becomes a delightful game, illustrating the contagious nature of positivity.

Planting Positivity Seeds

Transition to the gardening corner of our festival with the Planting Positivity Seeds game. Participants get hands-on as they plant small gardens or potted plants. Nurturing these green companions symbolizes personal growth, forging a beautiful connection between positivity and nature.

In this unconventional chapter, the standard learning structure is swapped for a festive atmosphere. Understanding positive thinking becomes as light and enjoyable as flying a colorful kite on a sunny day.

Dear villagers, let's embrace these game-centered chapters with open hearts. In the realm where sorrows have an end, let's dance with joy and integrate positive thinking as an interactive, vibrant aspect of our daily lives. Through play, we'll discover that the true essence of learning lies in the laughter echoing long after the games conclude

chapter 7. Navigating with Dignity

Under the venerable banyan tree, let's unravel the mid-point of our village odyssey - a pivotal chapter titled "Blossoming Souls." Here, the essence of positive thinking takes root in the fertile soil of respect, resonating with the simple yet profound truth: "Respect the Poor."

In this chapter, we immerse ourselves in stories that plumb the depths of the human spirit, unveiling the transformative power of positive thinking in the face of adversity. It's not about grandiose gestures or ostentatious displays; it's about discovering strength in simplicity and honoring the inherent dignity in every soul.

Ananya's Dignity

Ananya, a woman of resilience adorned in threadbare clothes, with a heart as pure as gold, imparts the wisdom that genuine dignity emanates from the way we carry ourselves, regardless of circumstances. Through the prism of positive thinking, she transformed daily struggles into stepping stones for personal growth, illustrating that self-respect can radiate as a guiding light for others.

chapter 8. The Village of Helping Hands

Our village emerges as a profound exemplar. Through the lens of positive thinking, villagers collectively redefined the perception of poverty. Respecting the poor wasn't a charitable act but a joyous celebration of shared humanity. It cultivated a community where every individual, irrespective of material possessions, was esteemed.

As we pause at this midpoint, let's reflect on these stories, delicate petals unfurling in the breeze. It's a moment to glean a profound comprehension of the transformative potency of positive thinking. When anchored in respect, positive thinking becomes a force that not only elevates the individual but also nurtures a community where each soul, be it affluent or humble, is acknowledged with dignity.

As we embark on the continuation of our journey, allow these stories to linger in our hearts, akin to the lingering fragrance of jasmine in the evening breeze. In the village where blossoming souls honor the dignity of each other, we acknowledge that positive thinking isn't solely a personal odyssey but a collective jubilation of humanity.

chapter 9. Navigating Obstacles with Respect

Amidst the gathered villagers under looming clouds, we step into the chapter titled "Stormy Skies, Steadfast Hearts." Here, we confront challenges that threaten to dim the light of positive thinking, with the unwavering mantra: "All Have Respect."

The Doubtful Shadows

Delve into the shadows that cast doubt on positive thinking, suggesting it's reserved for those with a charmed life. Address these concerns with the steadfast reminder that respect for oneself and others forms a powerful shield against doubts.

The Rain of Criticism

Navigate the rain of criticism that occasionally pours down on those choosing the path of positive thinking. Emphasize that respecting others' opinions doesn't equate to surrendering to negativity. It's a dance in the rain, where respect becomes an umbrella against the storms of criticism.

Strategies to Overcome Negativity:

Respectful Reflection:

Encourage villagers to engage in respectful self-reflection. Instead of harsh self-criticism, let them acknowledge their feelings, understanding that facing challenges is acceptable. This self-respect becomes the initial step towards maintaining a positive mindset.

chapter 10.Embrace Differences with Respect:

Foster an environment celebrating differences. When confronted with negativity from others, encourage villagers to respond with respect, recognizing that everyone carries their burdens. It's a reminder that respect, even in adversity, can be a potent tool for transformation.

Create a Circle of Support:

Urge villagers to build a circle of support. Surrounding oneself with those who uplift and respect one's journey provides strength during challenging times. A shared sense of respect within the community forms a collective shield against negativity.

As we navigate these stormy skies, let the village learn that respect isn't just a virtue; it's a formidable ally in the quest to maintain positive thinking. In the face of challenges, let us stand together, respecting the journey of each villager, recognizing that all have respect, and in that respect, we find the strength to weather any storm.

Over Despair with Strength and Respect

In the hushed embrace of the village night, we enter the chapter titled "Dawn After Darkness." Here, shadows cast doubt on the potency of positive thinking, and a whisper resonates through the village: "Enemy is Weak, Avoid Him."

chapter 11. Moment of Despair:

Illustrate a moment of profound despair, where the weight of challenges appears insurmountable. Villagers may feel the encroaching darkness, questioning whether positive thinking can genuinely be a guiding light in their darkest hours.

Stories of Triumph:

Introduce tales of individuals confronting seemingly insurmountable adversity. These stories will serve as beacons of hope, showcasing that even in the darkest nights, positive thinking can be a guiding star.

Arun's Resilience:

Share Arun's story, a villager who, amidst economic hardship, health struggles, and personal loss, found solace in positive thinking. Arun's journey becomes a testament to the strength within, emphasizing that avoiding despair is not a sign of weakness but a path to resilience.

chapter 12. Leela's Light:

Narrate Leela's tale, a woman combating internal demons and societal prejudices. Through positive thinking, she emerged from the shadows, embracing her worth and contributing to the village's well-being. Leela's story highlights that avoiding the enemy of self-doubt is a triumph in itself.

Strategies for Triumph:

Embrace Vulnerability with Strength:

Encourage villagers to embrace vulnerability as a source of strength. It's not about avoiding challenges but facing them with a heart fortified by positive thinking, understanding that acknowledging weakness is the first step to triumph.

Create a Path of Resilience:

Guide the villagers in forging a path of resilience. Share strategies for transforming setbacks into stepping stones, reinforcing the idea that avoiding despair doesn't mean ignoring challenges but navigating them with a resilient spirit.

As we navigate through the darkness, let the village learn that the enemy, in this case, is not positivity but the despair that seeks to engulf our spirits. In the stories of Arun, Leela, and others, we find the strength to avoid the enemy of despair, emerging into the dawn after darkness with the light of positive thinking

chapter 13. Light and Insight

As the village settles into the deep night, we enter the chapter titled "Guiding Stars in the Night." Here, we peer into the soul's darkest corners, recognizing that "Nothing Bad" is an absolute truth that transcends the shadows.

Depth of Personal Struggles:

Illuminate the personal struggles that cast a heavy shadow on maintaining a positive mindset. Share stories of villagers facing internal battles, grappling with self-doubt, and wrestling with the ghosts of the past.

Insights and Strategies:

The Lantern of Self-Compassion:

Encourage villagers to light the lantern of self-compassion. In the darkest moments, understanding that nobody is perfect and embracing one's flaws becomes a guiding light. Acceptance of oneself, even in the depth of struggles, is the first step toward a positive mindset.

Community Constellation:

SRINIVASA RAYA AND VILLAGE LIFE IS GOOD

Guide the villagers in forming a community constellation. In moments of darkness, seeking support from others and realizing that they, too, face their struggles, creates a shared tapestry of understanding. The village becomes a constellation of guiding stars, lighting the way through the darkest nights.

chapter 14.Celestial Vision of Hope:

Share the celestial vision of hope with the villagers. In the darkest hours, encourage them to look beyond the immediate struggles and envision a future filled with positivity. The ability to see hope as a guiding star, even in the darkest night, becomes a transformative force.

In this chapter, where shadows dance on the edges of the village, let the guiding stars of self-compassion, community support, and a celestial vision of hope lead the way. The villagers will learn that even in the darkest night of the soul, there exists a profound truth – that nothing bad is eternal, and with the right insights and strategies, the dawn is inevitable

The Goodness Within and Beyond

Under the first light of dawn, we enter the transformative chapter titled "Breaking Dawn." Here, the guiding principle echoes through the village: "Every is Only Good for Us."

Mastering Positive Thinking

This chapter serves as a bridge, a breaking dawn that signals the transition into the final part of our journey. The villagers have navigated challenges, faced personal struggles, and discovered the transformative power of positive thinking. Now, as the sun rises on a new day, it's time to delve deeper and master the art of positivity.

Embracing the Goodness Within:

Encourage the villagers to reflect on the goodness within themselves. Emphasize that, in the pursuit of mastering positive thinking, recognizing and embracing the inherent goodness within each villager becomes a foundation for personal growth and communal harmony.

chapter 15.Extending Goodness Beyond:

Guide the villagers in extending this goodness beyond themselves. Share stories of individuals who, having mastered positive thinking, became beacons of light for others. The notion that "Every is Only Good for Us" comes alive as villagers realize that their positive actions contribute to the well-being of the entire community.

Strategies for Mastery

Daily Affirmations:

Introduce the practice of daily affirmations. Villagers can start their day by acknowledging the goodness within themselves and affirming positive thoughts. This simple yet powerful ritual sets the tone for mastering positive thinking.

Acts of Kindness Campaign:

Initiate an Acts of Kindness Campaign within the village. By fostering a culture of kindness, villagers can experience firsthand the reciprocal nature of positivity

– how every positive action, no matter how small, contributes to the greater good.

Shared Gratitude Circle:

Encourage the creation of a Shared Gratitude Circle. Villagers can gather regularly to express gratitude for the positive moments in their lives, creating a shared energy that uplifts the entire community.

As we step into this breaking dawn, let the villagers understand that the principle of "Every is Only Good for Us" is not just a sentiment; it's a guiding philosophy for mastering positive thinking. In the chapters that follow, we will explore strategies and insights that lead to a profound mastery of positivity, both within ourselves and within the fabric of our village.

chapter 16. Ultimate Gifts of Mastery

As the sun climbs the sky, painting the village in hues of warmth, we enter the chapter titled "Radiant Horizons." Here, the ultimate truth is unveiled: "Don't Be Shame on Life."

Ultimate Benefits of Mastery:

Reveal the ultimate benefits that await those who master positive thinking. It's not just about fleeting moments of joy but the creation of a life that resonates with purpose, resilience, and an unwavering sense of well-being.

Success Stories:

Share success stories that echo through the village, weaving tales of individuals who, through the mastery of positive thinking, transformed their lives. Each story is a testament to the enduring impact positivity can have on personal growth, relationships, and overall life satisfaction.

Mira's Serenity:

Mira, once burdened by anxieties and self-doubt, found serenity through the mastery of positive thinking. Her story exemplifies how a tranquil mind and heart can weather life's storms with grace.

Rajiv's Ripple Effect:

Rajiv, inspired by the principles of positive thinking, became a catalyst for change in the village. His actions created a ripple effect, fostering a community where kindness, respect, and positivity flourished.

chapter 17. Long-Term Impact:

Delve into the long-term impact on individuals' lives. Beyond fleeting moments of happiness, mastering positive thinking becomes a cornerstone for a life filled with meaningful connections, personal fulfillment, and the ability to navigate challenges with resilience.

Don't Be Shame on Life:

Unpack the profound truth encapsulated in "Don't Be Shame on Life." Mastery of positive thinking is not about shying away from challenges or pretending life is always easy. It's about embracing life's complexities with courage, gratitude, and an unwavering belief that every experience, positive or negative, contributes to the rich tapestry of our existence.

As the villagers bask in the warmth of these radiant horizons, let them understand that the ultimate gifts of mastering positive thinking extend far beyond personal happiness. It's a transformative journey that paints the canvas of life with vibrant hues of purpose, resilience, and the unshakeable understanding that, in every moment, we have the

With the golden glow of the evening sun casting a warm embrace over the village, our journey culminates in the final chapter, "Wings of Victory." The canvas of positivity is adorned with the inspiring image: "You Are Only Born to Win, So Win Your Life."

In this tranquil landscape, where jasmine perfumes the air and laughter echoes through the village, we bid farewell on a note resounding with positivity. Life, we remind each villager, is a journey filled with victories waiting to be claimed – a tapestry woven with threads of resilience, gratitude, and the unwavering spirit of positive thinking.

As we conclude this transformative voyage, let the radiance of these final moments linger, not just as the end of a chapter but as the commencement of a lifelong celebration. The journey, we emphasize, doesn't conclude with the turning of the final page; it's an eternal blossoming of the soul, an ongoing exploration into the realms of positivity.

In this closing chapter, we extend a final call to action – a collective invitation to embrace the mantra "You Are Only Born to Win, So Win Your Life." These words, like a guiding star, beckon each villager to face challenges with confidence, celebrate triumphs with humility, and continue the journey of positive thinking with unwavering determination.

Picture the village uniting in a grand celebration beneath the moonlit sky, dancing to the harmonious melody of collective victories. The essence of triumph lies not only in personal accomplishments but in the shared spirit that flourishes when every villager embraces the power of positivity.

As the book concludes, let the image of wings of victory be etched in the hearts of the villagers. With these parting words, "You Are Only Born to Win, So Win Your Life," the village and the readers embark on a triumphant journey, knowing that the canvas of life is theirs to paint with the vibrant colors of positive thinking.

May each step forward be guided by the wings of victory, and may the echoes of positivity resonate eternally in the hearts of the villagers as they continue their journey into the boundless horizons of life's triumphs.

18.life in poverty of susma

Once upon a time, nestled in the heart of a lush valley, there was a quaint village named Susma. Despite facing the challenges of poverty, the spirit of the villagers illuminated the village like a beacon of hope.

Life in Susma was a testament to the resilience of its people. The villagers, though lacking material wealth, possessed an abundance of love, community spirit, and an unyielding determination to make the most of what they had. Every sunrise brought with it a new opportunity for unity and shared strength.

In the heart of Susma, there stood a communal gathering spot where villagers would convene to discuss their dreams and aspirations. This vibrant space became a symbol of their collective will to rise above their circumstances. It wasn't just a meeting place; it was a hub of creativity, where ideas blossomed like the flowers in the surrounding fields.

The villagers of Susma knew the true meaning of collaboration. They worked hand in hand, sharing whatever little they had, whether it was a handful of rice, a bundle of firewood, or a piece of wisdom passed down through generations. The sense of interconnectedness among them fostered a bond that poverty could not break.

Despite the scarcity of resources, the children of Susma reveled in the simplicity of their lives. They found joy in the laughter that echoed through the village, playing games with makeshift toys, and running through the meadows with the wind in their hair. Their innocence painted the village with colors of happiness, proving that true wealth lay in the intangible treasures of life.

The women of Susma were the backbone of the community. With grace and determination, they worked tirelessly to sustain their families. Their hands, weathered by toil, weaved stories of perseverance and strength. Together, they transformed the act of cooking simple meals into a celebration of life, sharing stories and laughter around the communal fire.

As seasons changed and time marched on, Susma faced its fair share of hardships, but the villagers faced them head-on, fortified by their unwavering sense of community. Each challenge was an opportunity for growth, and together they weathered the storms, emerging stronger and more united.

In the heart of Susma, poverty was not a shackle but a catalyst for resilience and communal harmony. The village, with its warm-hearted inhabitants, painted a beautiful portrait of a life rich in the things that truly matter – love, companionship, and the unbreakable bonds of a community that faced adversity with a smile, proving that even in the face of scarcity, the human spirit can thrive.

19.break down of winning

Certainly! Here's a breakdown of the positive elements that contribute to the winning atmosphere in the story of Susma:

Resilience and Determination:

Despite facing poverty, the villagers of Susma display unwavering determination and resilience.

They tackle challenges head-on, turning obstacles into opportunities for growth.

Community Spirit:

The villagers of Susma come together in a communal space, fostering a strong sense of community spirit.

Collaboration is a key theme, with villagers sharing resources, ideas, and supporting each other.

Creativity and Innovation:

The communal gathering spot becomes a hub of creativity where ideas flourish, showcasing the villagers' innovative spirit.

Despite limited resources, they find inventive ways to improve their lives and make the most of what they have.

Unity and Interconnectedness:

The sense of unity among the villagers is a prevailing theme.

Interconnectedness is emphasized as the villagers work hand in hand, sharing not just material possessions but also wisdom and experiences.

Joy in Simplicity:

The children find joy in the simplicity of their lives, emphasizing that happiness can be derived from the little things.

Play, laughter, and innocence are highlighted as integral components of the villagers' lives.

Strength in Women:

The women of Susma are portrayed as the backbone of the community, showcasing strength and grace.

Their resilience and hard work contribute significantly to the well-being of the village.

Transformation of Challenges:

Challenges are viewed as opportunities for growth, symbolizing the villagers' positive mindset.

Adversity is faced collectively, with the community emerging stronger and more united after each trial.

Appreciation for Intangible Wealth:

The story emphasizes that true wealth lies in intangible treasures such as love, companionship, and communal bonds.

The villagers find richness in their relationships and shared experiences.

Celebration of Life:

Everyday activities, such as cooking simple meals, become celebrations of life in Susma.

The villagers find joy in the present moment and cherish the shared experiences.

Human Spirit Triumphs:

The overarching theme is that the human spirit can thrive even in the face of poverty.

Susma exemplifies the idea that a positive mindset and a strong sense of community can elevate the human experience.

In summary, the winning elements in the story of Susma revolve around the strength, unity, and resilience of its community, emphasizing that true wealth is found in the richness of human connections and the ability to face challenges with a positive outlook.

20. villagers encorgment

Certainly! Here's a passage emphasizing the encouragement within the village of Susma:

"In the heart of Susma, encouragement flowed through the veins of the village like a gentle stream, nourishing the spirits of its inhabitants. Every challenge faced by the villagers became an opportunity for communal support and uplifting words. In the communal gathering space, where dreams were shared and ideas took root, encouragement echoed in every conversation.

As the sun dipped below the horizon, casting a warm glow on the faces gathered around the communal fire, the elders would share tales of resilience and triumph. Their words were not just stories but beacons of encouragement, guiding the younger generation through the sometimes rocky terrain of life.

The village echoed with the laughter of children, their playful spirit fueled by the encouragement of a community that believed in their potential. Each game played in the meadows became a lesson in perseverance, with cheers and words of affirmation ringing in the air. The elders, with their weathered hands and wisdom etched into every line on their faces, took joy in passing on encouragement like a cherished heirloom.

In times of hardship, when the weight of poverty seemed particularly heavy, the women of Susma gathered around the communal fire, exchanging words of strength and solidarity. Their encouragement was not just spoken; it was woven into the fabric of the community, creating a tapestry of support that could withstand any storm.

The encouragement in Susma was not limited to grand gestures; it was found in the everyday interactions, the shared glances that conveyed understanding, and the simple words that carried the weight of belief. In this village, encouragement was the invisible thread that bound hearts together, creating a tapestry of hope that adorned the very soul of Susma. It was a reminder that, no matter the circumstances, the village stood united, ready to uplift one another with the power of encouragement."

22.problems of ever family

Every family faces its own unique set of challenges, and while these challenges can vary widely, some common problems that many families encounter include:

Communication Issues:

Lack of effective communication can lead to misunderstandings, conflict, and a breakdown in relationships within the family.

Financial Strain:

Economic difficulties, debt, and financial instability can create stress and tension within a family, impacting overall well-being.

Parenting Challenges:

Raising children comes with its own set of challenges, including discipline issues, differing parenting styles, and the constant juggling of work and family responsibilities.

Conflict and Disagreements:

Differences in opinions, values, and personalities can lead to conflicts within a family, requiring effective conflict resolution strategies.

Work-Life Balance:

Balancing work commitments with family time can be a struggle, leading to feelings of neglect and frustration among family members.

Health Concerns:

Illness or health issues affecting a family member can be emotionally and financially draining, impacting the entire family's dynamics.

Crisis and Trauma:

Unexpected events, such as accidents, loss of a job, or natural disasters, can create crisis situations that families must navigate together.

Substance Abuse:

Substance abuse issues, whether it involves alcohol or drugs, can have a profound impact on family relationships and stability.

Cultural or Generational Differences:

Differing cultural backgrounds or generational gaps can contribute to misunderstandings and conflicts within a family.

Mental Health Challenges:

Mental health issues affecting one or more family members can strain relationships and require understanding and support.

Loss and Grief:

Coping with the loss of a loved one can be an emotionally challenging experience, and grieving processes may differ among family members.

Divorce and Separation:

Marital problems, divorce, or separation can create a significant upheaval in the family structure, affecting both parents and children.

Technology and Screen Time:

Excessive use of technology and screens can impact family interactions, leading to a sense of disconnection among family members.
Educational Challenges:
Supporting children through their educational journey, dealing with academic pressures, and addressing learning difficulties can be challenging for families.

It's important to note that while families may face these challenges, many also find ways to overcome them, grow stronger together, and foster a supportive and loving environment. Seeking professional help, open communication, and a willingness to work together can contribute to addressing and resolving these problems.

23.villan can change in village

In the heart of every village, there exists the potential for transformation, and even a perceived "villain" can undergo a change that not only alters their own path but also influences the entire community. Let's explore a narrative where a character in the village undergoes a significant transformation:

In the serene village of Elmridge, nestled between rolling hills and fertile fields, there was a man named Tobias. Known for his gruff demeanor and aloof behavior, Tobias had long been considered the village recluse. His interactions were limited to stern glances and curt responses, earning him the reputation of the village's reluctant villain.

However, beneath the rough exterior, there existed a story untold, wounds unhealed. Tobias had weathered his fair share of life's storms, and the weight of his past choices burdened him. The villagers, though wary of him, couldn't help but wonder about the man behind the facade.

One day, a series of events unfolded that would alter the course of Tobias's life. A new family arrived in Elmridge, seeking refuge from a nearby town. They were met with apprehension and skepticism, as the villagers feared the stranger among them. Tobias, initially indifferent, observed the newcomers from a distance.

As days turned into weeks, Tobias found himself unintentionally drawn into the family's struggles. He witnessed their determination to build a new life, their resilience in the face of adversity. Slowly, the icy walls around his heart began to thaw.

A crisis struck the village when a sudden storm threatened to destroy the crops, the lifeblood of Elmridge. The villagers, faced with the imminent threat of famine, rallied together to save their livelihoods. Unexpectedly, Tobias emerged as a silent force, utilizing his knowledge of the land to guide the community.

His actions spoke louder than any words could have, and the villagers started to see a different side of Tobias. They began to understand the pain he carried, the wounds of a past that had shaped him into the person they once feared. Compassion replaced judgment, and the village realized that even the coldest hearts could warm in the presence of understanding.

Tobias's transformation became a symbol of redemption for Elmridge. The once-perceived villain had become a guardian, a mentor, and an integral part of the village's collective story. His journey of change taught everyone that, within the heart of even the most guarded soul, there lies the potential for growth, forgiveness, and the renewal of community bonds.

In the end, Elmridge thrived not only because of the crops saved from the storm but because the village itself had grown richer in empathy, unity, and the profound understanding that everyone, no matter their past, had the capacity for change.

24. no one is bad in village

In the idyllic village of Harmony Haven, a remarkable phenomenon existed - a place where the concept of being 'bad' was an anomaly. This quaint village was a living testament to the power of understanding, compassion, and a shared commitment to the well-being of every resident.

Harmony Haven was founded on principles of unity and empathy, with each villager embracing the notion that everyone carried a unique story. There was no room for judgment, only space for acceptance and support.

In this utopian village, challenges and conflicts were not viewed as a result of 'bad' intentions, but rather as opportunities for growth and communal understanding. When disagreements arose, the villagers would gather in a designated space called the "Circle of Compassion," a place where open dialogue and active listening were the norms.

The residents of Harmony Haven believed that everyone had inherent goodness within them, and any negative actions were merely manifestations of unmet needs or unresolved issues. When someone faced difficulties, the community rallied together to offer assistance, guidance, and emotional support.

The village school was not just a place for academic learning but also a hub for emotional intelligence and conflict resolution. Children were taught the art of understanding and expressing their feelings, fostering an environment where empathy flourished from a young age.

Even in moments of adversity, the villagers of Harmony Haven displayed unwavering kindness. Instead of labeling individuals as 'bad,' they sought to understand the root causes of behavior and address them with collective compassion. Restorative justice practices were employed, focusing on healing and rehabilitation rather than punitive measures.

The absence of judgment allowed the villagers to embrace diversity wholeheartedly. Differences in backgrounds, beliefs, and perspectives were celebrated, fostering a rich tapestry of experiences that contributed to the vibrant tapestry of Harmony Haven.

In this village where no one was considered 'bad,' the very fabric of community life was woven with threads of acceptance, forgiveness, and an unwavering belief in the inherent goodness of each individual. Harmony Haven stood as a living example that, with understanding and compassion, a community could create a haven where the notion of being 'bad' was rendered obsolete.

25.village is greater than city

The debate over whether a village is greater than a city or vice versa often depends on individual preferences, lifestyle choices, and perspectives. Here are some reasons why some might argue that a village is greater than a city:

Community and Social Bonds:

Villages are often characterized by close-knit communities where everyone knows each other. There is a strong sense of belonging and shared responsibility, fostering deep social bonds.

Peaceful and Tranquil Environment:

Villages generally offer a quieter and more peaceful environment compared to the hustle and bustle of a city. The natural surroundings, open spaces, and slower pace of life contribute to a serene atmosphere.

Closer to Nature:

Villages are often situated in rural areas surrounded by nature. Residents can enjoy cleaner air, open landscapes, and a closer connection to the natural world.

Less Stressful Lifestyle:

The slower pace of life in villages is often associated with reduced stress levels. There's less traffic, noise, and the overall lifestyle tends to be more relaxed.

Cost of Living:

In many cases, the cost of living in villages is lower than in cities. Housing, food, and other essentials may be more affordable, allowing residents to maintain a simpler and potentially more sustainable lifestyle.

Cultural Richness:

Villages often have a rich cultural heritage and traditions that are preserved over generations. This cultural authenticity can provide a sense of continuity and identity.

Personal Space and Privacy:

Villages typically offer more personal space and privacy compared to the closely packed living arrangements often found in cities.

Less Pollution:

With fewer industrial activities and traffic, villages tend to have lower levels of pollution, contributing to better air quality and overall environmental health.

Local Agriculture and Fresh Produce:

Villages are often closer to agricultural areas, allowing residents to access fresh and locally produced food. There may be a stronger connection to farming practices and seasonal eating.

Easier Access to Outdoor Activities:

Villages are often surrounded by natural landscapes, providing easy access to outdoor activities such as hiking, fishing, or simply enjoying the countryside.

While some may argue that villages are greater, it's important to note that cities also offer numerous advantages, such as diverse cultural opportunities, educational institutions, advanced healthcare, and a wider range of job opportunities. Ultimately, whether a village or city is deemed greater depends on individual preferences and priorities.

Life in a village and life in a city present contrasting experiences shaped by different environments, lifestyles, and opportunities. Here's a comparison between the two:

26.Life in a Village:

Community and Social Connections:

Villages are characterized by close-knit communities where everyone tends to know each other. There's a strong sense of community and mutual support.

Simplicity and Tranquility:

Village life is often associated with simplicity and a slower pace. The environment is generally quieter, and residents enjoy a more tranquil atmosphere surrounded by nature.

Close to Nature:

Villages are usually situated in rural areas, offering a closer connection to nature. Residents may experience cleaner air, open spaces, and a peaceful environment.

Agricultural Lifestyle:

Many villagers are engaged in agriculture, either as farmers or supporting agricultural activities. The lifestyle is closely tied to the land and seasonal cycles.

Limited Access to Amenities:

Villages may have limited access to modern amenities such as healthcare facilities, educational institutions, and entertainment options.

Tight-knit Culture:

Villages often have a rich cultural heritage, and traditions are preserved over generations. There's a strong sense of cultural identity and continuity.

Personal Space:

Residents in villages typically have more personal space, and homes are often surrounded by open land.

Less Hectic Lifestyle:

The rhythm of life in a village is usually less hectic, allowing for more leisure time and a greater focus on relationships and community.

Life in a City:

Diverse Opportunities:

Cities offer a wide range of opportunities for employment, education, and cultural experiences. There's often a diversity of industries and job sectors.

Urban Amenities:

Cities are equipped with advanced infrastructure, including healthcare facilities, educational institutions, shopping centers, and entertainment options.

Fast-paced Lifestyle:

Life in a city tends to be more fast-paced, with busy schedules, traffic, and a high level of activity. People often have demanding jobs and hectic social lives.

Cultural Diversity:

Cities are melting pots of different cultures, languages, and traditions. This diversity contributes to a rich cultural tapestry and a variety of culinary and artistic experiences.

Advanced Services:

Access to advanced healthcare, transportation, and technology services is more readily available in cities.

Educational Opportunities:

Cities often house prestigious educational institutions, providing a wide range of academic and career opportunities.

Increased Pollution:

The concentration of industrial and vehicular activities in cities can lead to higher levels of pollution compared to rural areas.

Diverse Culinary Scene:

Cities boast diverse culinary offerings, with restaurants featuring international cuisines.

In essence, the choice between village and city life depends on individual preferences, priorities, and lifestyle goals. Some may find fulfillment in the simplicity and community of village life, while others may thrive in the dynamic and diverse environment of a city.

27.sports in village life

Sports play a crucial role in fostering a positive and healthy life in villages. Here are several ways in which sports contribute to the well-being and development of individuals and communities in rural areas:

Physical Fitness:

Engaging in sports promotes physical fitness and well-being. Regular physical activity helps combat sedentary lifestyles, obesity, and related health issues, contributing to a healthier community.

Team Building and Social Bonding:

Team sports, such as soccer, cricket, or volleyball, provide opportunities for social interaction and team building. Playing together fosters a sense of camaraderie and strengthens community bonds.

Community Engagement:

Sports events and tournaments become focal points for community engagement. Villagers come together to support and participate in local matches, creating a vibrant and inclusive social atmosphere.

Skill Development:

Participation in sports helps individuals develop a variety of skills, including teamwork, leadership, communication, and decision-making. These skills are transferable to various aspects of life.

Health Awareness:

Through sports activities, communities become more aware of the importance of health and fitness. Health-related workshops and awareness programs can be integrated into sports events to educate villagers about healthy living.

Empowerment and Inclusivity:

Sports provide a platform for empowerment, irrespective of age, gender, or socio-economic status. Inclusive sports programs ensure that everyone in the village can participate and benefit from the positive aspects of physical activity.

Youth Development:

Engaging youth in sports helps channel their energy positively. It provides an alternative to negative influences and promotes discipline, responsibility, and a sense of purpose.

Cultural Celebrations:

Traditional sports and games specific to the culture of the village can be incorporated into celebrations and festivals. This not only preserves cultural heritage but also adds an element of fun and excitement to community events.

Infrastructure Development:

The need for sports facilities can drive infrastructure development in villages. Building playgrounds, courts, or sports fields not only supports sports activities but also enhances the overall infrastructure of the community.

Conflict Resolution:

Sports competitions offer a healthy outlet for competition and can serve as a means of resolving conflicts or differences within the community. It encourages fair play and mutual respect.

Mental Health Benefits:

Regular physical activity through sports has positive effects on mental health. It reduces stress, anxiety, and depression, contributing to overall well-being.

Skill Transfer for Livelihood:

Some sports involve skills that can be transferred to livelihood activities. For example, teamwork and discipline learned through team sports can be valuable in various professional settings.

In conclusion, sports in villages contribute significantly to the physical, social, and mental well-being of individuals and communities. The positive impact goes beyond the playing field, influencing various aspects of village life and fostering a healthier, more connected, and empowered community.

28.encourgment among villagers

Encouragement among villagers is a powerful force that builds a resilient and supportive community. Here are ways in which encouragement thrives in a village setting:

Collective Celebrations:

Villagers come together to celebrate individual and community achievements, creating an environment where success is shared and applauded.

Community Recognition:

Public acknowledgment of efforts and accomplishments, whether big or small, fosters a sense of pride and encouragement. This recognition can be done through community events or informal gatherings.

Supportive Networks:

Villagers often form close-knit networks where individuals encourage one another. Whether it's in times of personal challenges or during communal projects, this support system is crucial for well-being.

Community Meetings:

Regular community meetings provide a platform for individuals to share their aspirations, goals, and challenges. In these settings, villagers offer words of encouragement, advice, and assistance.

Elders' Wisdom:

Elders in the village often play a role in offering guidance and encouragement to the younger generation. Their life experiences and wisdom become valuable sources of motivation.

Mentorship Programs:

Establishing mentorship programs within the village encourages experienced individuals to guide and support those who are seeking advice or facing challenges.

Education and Skill Enhancement:

Encouragement is often extended towards education and skill development. Villagers may support each other's pursuit of knowledge and acquiring new skills, recognizing the long-term benefits for the individual and the community.

Positive Reinforcement:

Emphasizing positive qualities and actions creates an atmosphere where individuals feel valued. Constructive feedback and positive reinforcement contribute to a culture of encouragement.

Shared Responsibilities:

Encouragement is embedded in the collaboration and shared responsibilities within the community. Whether it's a farming project, a cultural event, or infrastructure development, the collective effort is recognized and celebrated.

Inclusive Initiatives:

Encouragement is inclusive, ensuring that every villager, regardless of age, gender, or background, feels empowered and supported in their endeavors.

Festivals and Traditions:

Village festivals and traditions often incorporate elements of encouragement. These events become opportunities to highlight individual and collective achievements.

Open Communication:

A culture of open communication fosters encouragement. Villagers feel comfortable expressing their dreams and concerns, knowing that their voices will be heard and respected.

Volunteerism and Community Service:

Encouragement is evident in volunteering and community service efforts. Villagers supporting each other in philanthropic endeavors create a positive cycle of giving and receiving encouragement.

Youth Empowerment:

Special focus on encouraging the younger generation through educational initiatives, skill-building programs, and mentorship ensures the continuity of a supportive community.

Encouragement among villagers creates a nurturing environment where individuals feel motivated to pursue their goals, overcome challenges, and contribute positively to the community's growth and well-being. It forms the backbone of a resilient and thriving village

29.people live long reason

People live long lives due to a combination of factors, including advancements in healthcare, improved living conditions, better nutrition, and overall progress in public health. Here are several key reasons why people live longer:

Advancements in Medicine:

Medical breakthroughs, including vaccines, antibiotics, and advancements in surgical procedures, have played a crucial role in treating and preventing diseases, leading to increased life expectancy.

Access to Healthcare:

Improved accessibility to healthcare services, especially in urban areas, allows individuals to receive timely medical attention, preventive care, and ongoing treatment for chronic conditions.

Public Health Initiatives:

Public health campaigns, such as vaccination programs, disease prevention efforts, and awareness campaigns, contribute to reducing the prevalence of infectious diseases and promoting overall well-being.

Sanitation and Clean Water:

Better sanitation facilities and access to clean water help prevent the spread of waterborne diseases, contributing to improved health and longer life expectancy.

Nutrition and Food Security:

Increased awareness of nutrition, better agricultural practices, and improved food distribution contribute to a more stable and nourishing food supply, positively impacting health and longevity.

Education and Awareness:

SRINIVASA RAYA AND VILLAGE LIFE IS GOOD

Increased education and awareness about health, hygiene, and disease prevention empower individuals to make healthier lifestyle choices, leading to improved overall well-being.

Technology and Telemedicine:

Advancements in technology, including telemedicine and remote monitoring, enhance healthcare accessibility, particularly for individuals in remote or underserved areas.

Economic Development:

Economic progress is often associated with improved living standards, access to healthcare, and better education, all of which contribute to longer life expectancy.

Social Support Systems:

Strong social support networks, including family, friends, and community connections, play a role in mental and emotional well-being, which can impact overall health and longevity.

Stable Political Environment:

A stable political environment and social infrastructure contribute to better healthcare systems, public services, and overall societal well-being.

Decrease in Smoking Rates:

Awareness campaigns about the harmful effects of smoking and increased efforts to reduce tobacco use have contributed to a decline in smoking rates, leading to improved cardiovascular health.

Medical Research and Innovation:

Ongoing medical research and technological innovations continually introduce new treatments, medications, and therapies that enhance the ability to manage and treat various health conditions.

Improved Living Conditions:

Better housing, sanitation, and living conditions contribute to overall health and reduce the risk of infectious diseases and environmental hazards.

Genetic Factors:

Genetic predispositions to certain diseases and conditions also play a role in life expectancy, and ongoing research in genetics contributes to a better understanding of these factors.

The combination of these factors has led to a significant increase in life expectancy globally, with many people enjoying longer and healthier lives than in previous generations. Continued efforts in healthcare, public health, education, and technology are essential to further improve and sustain these positive trends

30.postivity is in village

Positivity in villages often stems from the close-knit communities, simplicity of life, and strong connections to nature. Here are several aspects contributing to positivity in village life:

Community Spirit:

Villages are known for their tight-knit communities where people often know each other. The sense of togetherness and shared experiences fosters a positive and supportive environment.

Cultural Richness:

Villages often have rich cultural traditions and celebrations. These events create a sense of unity and pride, contributing to the overall positivity within the community.

Simplicity of Life:

The slower pace of life in villages allows residents to appreciate the simple joys and moments. This emphasis on simplicity often leads to a more positive outlook.

Connection to Nature:

Villages are usually surrounded by natural landscapes. The proximity to nature, open spaces, and clean air contributes to a sense of well-being and positivity.

Collective Celebrations:

Villages often come together to celebrate festivals, harvests, and other communal events. These celebrations bring joy, strengthen bonds, and contribute to a positive community spirit.

Shared Responsibilities:

Villagers often collaborate on various tasks and projects. The shared responsibilities create a sense of belonging and accomplishment, fostering a positive community ethos.

Generational Connections:

Strong connections between different generations within a village provide a sense of continuity. The wisdom of elders and the energy of the youth contribute to a positive and balanced community dynamic.

Support Systems:

Villagers often form strong support networks. Whether it's helping in times of need, celebrating achievements, or offering emotional support, these networks enhance overall positivity.

Close Relationships:

Close relationships and friendships within the village contribute to a positive social atmosphere. The familiarity and trust among residents create a sense of security and well-being.

Resilience in Adversity:

Villagers often display resilience in the face of challenges. The collective effort to overcome difficulties fosters a positive mindset and a belief in the strength of the community.

Traditional Practices:

Engaging in traditional practices and customs can bring a sense of continuity and pride, contributing to the overall positivity within the community.

Emphasis on Values:

Villages often place importance on shared values such as cooperation, respect, and mutual support. These values contribute to a positive social environment.

Inclusive Atmosphere:

Villages tend to be more inclusive, where everyone has a role to play. This inclusivity fosters positive interactions and a sense of belonging.

Appreciation for Local Resources:

SRINIVASA RAYA AND VILLAGE LIFE IS GOOD

Villagers often appreciate and make the most of local resources. This sustainable approach to living can contribute to a positive relationship with the environment.

In summary, positivity in villages arises from the sense of community, connection to nature, cultural richness, and the emphasis on shared values. These factors create an environment where individuals feel supported, connected, and optimistic about their lives and the future of their community.

www.ingramcontent.com/pod-product-compliance
Lightning Source LLC
Chambersburg PA
CBHW060758260726
48660CB00002B/686